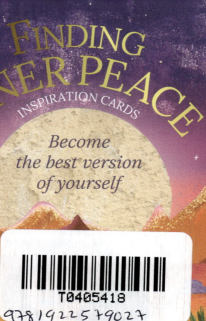

FINDING INNER PEACE

INSPIRATION CARDS

*Become
the best version
of yourself*

T0405418

9781922579027

livia burki

Introduction

Hello and welcome. If you are looking for the motivation and inspiration you need to lead a self-determined and healthful life physically and mentally you have come to the right place. The 36 inspirational *Finding Inner Peace* cards were created to help you understand it doesn't matter what your past is or at what point in life you are, you can always look ahead and take control of your life.

To know that nothing is permanent and to realise you can completely recreate yourself if you wish to is a gift; all that really matters are the decisions you make today. This compact and aesthetically illustrated deck will support you in your personal and spiritual growth.

We all have dark and light sides, and the message here is to embrace both sides of your personality and find a balance between the two extremes, even though it may at times be a struggle to do so. To have been through the most distressing pain and to know the deepest abyss of your soul doesn't mean you can't be happy. What it does mean is that you will appreciate every moment of happiness so much more intensely.

How to use the cards

The *Finding Inner Peace* cards are divided into four sections, which are outlined below. Pick one card each day from any of the sections to act as a focus for motivation and understanding and as a reminder to be kind to and appreciative of yourself.

...ady to rise up: you realise something is wrong, that you are dissatisfied with yourself. Things that used to make you happy no longer feel right. Perhaps there are people in your life who are holding you back. You recognise this and want to change your life, and the cards in this section will help you take the first steps forward and show you that fall-backs are not a reason to give up – they help you to grow.

Light is wrapping me: change can be painful and difficult, but the love you have for yourself is big enough to block everything that stands in the way of your serendipity. The light that has always been within you is redeveloping its power and warmly supports you on your journey and shows you how to treat yourself with love.

Growing to my fullest potential: your thoughts are potent. The more positive they are the more positive things will happen in your life, so get over your ego and utilise this power. Become more and more aware of how much your body and soul react to external influences. In this phase of your journey you should be able to react to your environment with a little more understanding and acceptance. The cards in this section will help you to strengthen your focus and believe in yourself.

Welcome change and welcome home: open your heart and mind to receive warmth and love. Surround yourself with people who are good to you, and who respect and accept you. Live your life in self-reflection and be the change you want to see in the world. Appreciate your true self, your soul. The cards in this section should remind you that you are totally free from everything that holds you back, so you can live a life of full authenticity.

Ready to rise up

1. Becoming aware

I am becoming aware of things that are holding me back so I can live my life to its full potential.

Self-awareness is the key to improving your life, and being honest with yourself is the first step. Ask yourself what habits and thought patterns you have that are toxic. Understanding that you actually have choices and you're not stuck is a game changer.

2. Letting go

Now is the time to let go of everything that no longer serves me.

Look for whatever is triggering negativity and holding you back from living a fulfilled life and being happy. Sometimes the best favour you can do yourself is being radical in the changes you undertake. You don't have to please anyone, nor do you owe anyone anything; it's your well-being that is the most important.

3. Change is good

I am strong enough to give up bad habits. Change is for good and I have this.

Letting go of ideas, habits and people that were with you for a long time is not a simple thing. Choose a substitute for your vicious habits and surround yourself with people who live the way you want to live. It will get easier with every little step you take and every success you experience.

4. Transformation

Parts of my transformation might be uncomfortable, but I have the power to go through this.

You have already achieved a lot by having a strong mindset and knowing your 'why'. Remember that healing takes time, and transformation is happening now if things are starting to make you feel uncomfortable. And at the end it's not about being perfect; it's your motivation and the effort you make that will pay off.

5. I have choices

I don't have to be stuck in something that no longer fits. I have choices: always.

Sometimes you forget that you can choose. You have the privilege of selecting what job you want to do and what you say and think. If your life doesn't make you feel excited, you have the option of changing it. Choose yourself, and opt for a compelling future.

6. Creating new habits

I am strong enough to turn bad practices into good habits. I am the creator of my own life.

It's not all about restrictions. When you begin to avoid toxic habits you will find there is suddenly a lot of time and space for other activities. Think about things you liked doing when you were a child, resume an old hobby or look for a new one, start a gratitude journal or connect with nature: there are so many options.

7. Patience pays off

I'm patient because I know I am going through a process and am in full acceptance of the situation.

You will block your progress when you are impatient with yourself. It's okay to occasionally go backwards and humanly experience challenges. Be kind to yourself, as the challenges are part of your journey. It's important to treat yourself as you want others to treat you because self-love is the key to living a satisfied life.

8. A new day; a new start

It's okay to fail. Every day is a new start and I will treat myself graciously.

You can rise up from literally anything. When you wake up in the morning, soak up the fresh energy and the new opportunities and decide to be thankful and positive. Thinking about a bad yesterday is useless; the past is gone and today is full of possibilities. Let it go and start anew.

9. Don't look back

I may be feeling nostalgic about several things in my past, but I know I have the power to move forward.

Romanticising a toxic habit or relationship can elicit bittersweet feelings, but it's nothing more than self-sabotage. You no longer need these things, as you're about to win so much more. Listen to your inner positive voice, act like your higher self and focus on the improvements in your life.

Light is wrapping me

10. It has always been within

Everything I need is already inside me, as it has always been.
The light inside you will shine brighter with each step you take; it will guide you to become the person you were always meant to be. Nothing and no one can overcome this light, and you will discover endless peace and warmth if you just learn to connect with it again.

11. I am worthy

I deserve more than just a comfortable and easy life. I am worthy of so much more.
You will feel your self-esteem growing when you reconnect with your true self. You will realise you have the power to live a life that really makes you excited every morning when you wake up. It's time to leave your comfort zone and start dreaming big.

12. Being gentle with myself

I'm gentle with myself and make happiness in my life a priority.
Take the time you need to invest in yourself, whether this means meditating, finding a personal coach who excites you or spoiling yourself with a bunch of flowers. Also, be kinder towards others as it will impact the way you think about and treat yourself. The world needs more humanity.

13. Unbecoming everything I'm not

I'm not changing for anything or anyone. I'm celebrating pure authenticity and unbecoming everything I am not.

Follow your intuition and stop aiming to please others or comparing yourself to them. Appreciate who you are and stand up for your values. From now on there doesn't have to be a difference between who you are and what you do; express your individuality and celebrate your uniqueness.

14. Honouring my inner light

The times when I let my brightness dim are over. I fully honour my inner light.

You've made mistakes just like everyone else and you will certainly have regrets, but it's time to forgive yourself and possibly others as well and to be proud of yourself. You are trying hard and you've come so far; just having the will to work on yourself and your personal growth is honourable. You are wonderful: never forget that!

15. Love awakens my soul

I will begin to truly love myself with a love that awakens my soul. My heart is open to giving and receiving love.

It's not just a cliché: the more loving care you give to yourself the more love you have to give to others and the more love you will get back. Self-love is one of the best things you can do for yourself if you wish to live a joyful life. Working with and taking care of your inner child is a good way to improve self-love and is the key to confidence.

16. My body is a temple

The love I have for my body is growing more and more. It is the temple of my soul and must be treated well.

Your mind and spirit work together with your body, so it's important to be appreciative of what your body can do for you. Nurture it with good food, listen to it, challenge it and let it rest. Be nice to your body and it will be nice to you.

17. Nurturing my soul

Growth on all levels is a priority, so I will take the time to nurture my soul with wisdom and positivity.

Find some space and time to quieten your mind and ask yourself what you need at this point in your life. Taking the time to meditate can help you a lot: it's such a simple tool but it is very impactful. It is not selfish to put your needs first and, in fact, it is essential and necessary. Start to nourish your soul with happy thoughts and positive energy.

18. Energy protection

I have the power to protect my energy and maintain a positive attitude. No one can destroy my inner peace.

When it comes to energy protection, it's all about intention and how you react to certain people or situations: you're going to attract more of whatever you focus on. You have to take responsibility for your reactions to the negativity of the people around you, as you can decide to not allow someone else's energy to affect you.

Growing to my fullest potential

19. It's time to heal and evolve

I'm taking care of myself and my inner child and filling my mind with light-filled thoughts. I will fully heal and evolve.

To become a happy and successful human being you need to listen to your inner child. Turn inward and have a close and honest look at what still has to heal. It is only when you are at peace with yourself and your past that you will be able to become the best version of yourself.

20. Quietening my ego

My ego is no longer taking control of my life. Rather, I allow my higher self to guide me.

Your ego is not useless because it helps you to take initiative, have goals and stand up for your rights. However, it shouldn't dominate but rather should be about balancing your values, needs and aims and having the strength to ask for what you need in a way that is also good for others. Listen more to the voice of your higher self.

21. Appreciating myself

I completely know my own worth and honour and love my wonderful soul.

You have to truly believe in yourself because no one is going to if you don't, and you really must understand that you are a good person and deserve to be treated with respect. Appreciate yourself and you will see great possibilities appearing in your life.

22. Softening my heart

I'm no longer willing to let bad experiences take over my heart. It's time to let go of negativity.

Everyone experiences bad things in life, some more so than others, but how you handle those instances is up to you. You can use them to grow and be even more generous, and open your heart to all the magic that can happen in your life if you just allow it.

23. Having sympathy and acceptance

I protect Mother Earth and have sympathy and acceptance for all living creatures.

Be more aware of the responsibility you have to protect Gaia and all of the creatures living on earth. Be conscious of what you consume and the footprint you leave. Every one of us should live a life of peace and be in harmony with the wildlife on the planet.

24. My thoughts are powerful

As I am aware of the power of my thoughts, I am able to create my dream life.

To change the external, you must first change the internal. When you use the immense power of your thoughts, you will be able to affect what happens to you. Whatever you desire you can achieve through mind power. Do yourself a favour: observe your thoughts and make sure they are positive.

25. Travelling

Travelling opens my mind and raises my self-development to new levels.

Experiencing something new in a place you aren't familiar with will have a huge impact on your personal growth and happiness, as it will give you fresh perspectives and confidence. You will be able to better reflect on yourself and discover what you really want and need in life. Seek opportunities to take a trip somewhere by yourself.

26. Believing in new beginnings

I am the director of my life and understand the healing power of new beginnings.

Every day you get the chance for a new beginning, and a better day begins with a better start. You can choose whether or not today is going to be a new day or a recycled day. By implementing good intentions every day, you proactively make use of the power of fresh beginnings.

27. Focusing is key

I can handle setbacks and use them to grow.
Focusing helps me to achieve everything I desire.

Focusing on your spirituality allows you to see beyond a setback and find a purpose for it. Part of improving your mental focus concerns making the most of the resources you have available. Stop multitasking and instead give your full attention to one thing at a time.

Welcome change and welcome home

28. Rediscovering myself

My true self is showing up more and more. Who I am and what I do is confirmed day after day.

Authenticity is not about your image but is about staying true to what you believe. It is about being true to yourself through your thoughts, words and actions. Strive to be the best person you can be with both your limitations and strengths.

29. Opening my mind

I open my mind to the love, wisdom and guidance of the universe and I will learn to trust again.

It's not always easy to trust you are on the right path and that everything will work out for the best, so you try to control circumstances or force things. However, sometimes you need to allow things to unfold as they will, so it's time to have faith in the universe's guidance.

30. I am blooming

I am full of authenticity because I bloom exactly the way I was always meant to.

It's never too late to live your purpose, and by acknowledging your weaknesses you have already made a big step. Never give up, because you never know what you can miss if you do. If you give life a chance it will surprise you in positive ways.

31. Visualising my wildest dreams

I know the power of my thoughts, and visualising them will lead me to live the life of my wildest dreams.

Creating a personal vision board is a very powerful way to visualise your dreams and goals. As you regularly look at it, you both consciously and subconsciously remind yourself of your intentions and will push towards them. It's also a great way to emotionally, energetically and creatively connect with your goals.

32. Having a healthy lifestyle

I am conscious of the force of nutritious food and know that a healthy lifestyle is not just a trend but is fundamental for a happy life.

A healthy body means a healthy mind, and the clearer your mind is the easier it will be to achieve your goals. A clear mind will improve your mood and provide the energy and drive you need to live to your full potential, so get started now and stay motivated.

33. Being loud and powerful

I'm maintaining my standards and ideals, and I'm proudly loud and powerful about them.

You don't have to accept everything that comes your way, so learn when to say 'No'. Begin standing up for your rights without hurting others, and don't wait for opportunities to come to you. Rather, be brave enough to make the first move and create your own opportunities.

34. My lifetime dreams

I don't have to dream my life, as I have the power to manifest my lifetime dreams.

Write down your dreams and end with the words, 'My life will be like this or better, to the highest welfare of all.' Visualise what your life will look like when you achieve your dreams, and feel as though you already have what you want. Take action to help the universe make what you wish for happen.

35. Spiritual awakening

I will cultivate mindfulness every day so my vibration rises to a spiritual awakening.

It is time to let your higher self rise, to become more calm, neutral, compassionate, understanding and intuitive. Shadow work helps to uproot secretly held beliefs, such as that you're better than others, and to overcome the characteristics of a loud ego.

36. Embracing my beautiful soul

Being truly myself is the biggest gift I can offer myself and others. I embrace my beautiful soul and show it to the world.

Lovingly look at yourself and accept all of your beauty but also the things you like to a lesser extent. Without an unconditional acceptance of all that you are, there can be no experience of true self-love and authenticity. If you refuse to also accept your faults, you refuse the opportunity to grow – but you are more than enough.

 About the author

Olivia Bürki is a Swiss freelance artist who is currently travelling the world to follow her true self. Her passion is illustrating with spiritual, bohemian and nature themes that always have a floral and dreamy touch. She works in traditional and digital mediums and likes to combine both techniques in her work.

You can find Olivia at www.oliviabuerki.com or on Instagram, @oliviabuerkidesign.